Kid's Guide to Life with Food Allergies

For Kids, By Kids

BY KAI BROWN

Published in the U.S.A

First Edition September 2017

Edited By:

Michael Brown, Cassandra Quick, Emi Brown, and Cynthia Nishimoto

Table of Contents

THIS BOOK IS DEDICATED TO EVERY KID STRUGGLING WITH

ALLERGIES AROUND THE WORLD

SPECIAL THANKS TO PREMIER SUPPORTERS ON KICKSTARTER:

Brett Baker, Byron Nutley,
Cynthia Stein, Doug Christel,
Don Hyun, Keiko Berry,
Robert Campbell, Roger Holcombe,
Viet An Ly

THANKS TO $50+ SUPPORTERS ON KICKSTARTER:

Andy Dills, Cinda Cates, Darlene Hamilton, Ed Whatley, Jeri Jarvie, Kerry Sullivan, Katie Bryan, Lauren Campbell, Linda Brown, Lisa Wyler, Petina Jordan, Sarah Chudy, Sarah Jones, Sean Gordon, Shou-Ching Schilling, Tami Armster, Tina Weber

THANKS TO OTHERS THAT SUPPORTED ME ON KICKSTARTER:

Barbara Berghammer, Brett Kassel, Carolyn Blaylock, Christine Stonier, Colleen Nishimoto, Dan Lowe, Deanna Ableser, Erin Swanson, Erna Barenio, Gus Bornstein, Javier Garay, Jennifer Bowen, Julie Falter, Rebecca Squires, Missy Klemin, Heather Sachs, Rachael Anne, Matt Dahlberg, Meredith Makin, Michelle Youness, Miki Kasahara, Oliver Brossman, Ryan Hoffman, Sally Somsel, Tasia Arnold, Tokiko Poppe

4

Join the KFAN family on Twitter @kidsfanorg

Visit us at http://kidsfan.org

PRELUDE

INTRODUCTION

Hi, everyone! Thanks for taking the time to read my book! My name is Kai Brown. I'm twelve years old; soon to be thirteen. I'm severely allergic to all peanuts and tree nuts, but you could never tell by looking at me—unless I'm having a reaction, of course. The reason I'm writing this book is to help other kids with food allergies understand that they aren't alone, to share some of my stories and habits, to discuss allergy-related developments in medical science, and to inform others about interesting facts related to allergies. I'm writing about these issues all from a kid's perspective.

Food Allergies are a medical condition where exposure to food can trigger a harmful reaction in the body. This response is called an *allergic reaction*. Your immune system attacks proteins in the food that are normally safe for people to eat. We'll talk more about the immune system later.

Having allergies can cause people to treat you differently. Sometimes they're being mean like when classmates choose to bully people with food allergies. Sometimes they're trying to be nice like when people worry they are putting you in danger by eating something you're allergic to near you. For example, at my old school there was an allergen-free table, where you could only take two friends to sit next to you and only if they didn't have allergens in their lunch. I know it was to keep us safe, but it felt like we were separated and treated differently. It didn't make me feel safe, it made me feel different, in a bad way.

What I've learned when eating food is that no matter what

people say, you should **always** check the ingredients yourself because some people just don't know or understand how dangerous it can be for me. In addition, it's easy for someone to make a mistake when checking the labeling for you. Also, be very careful when checking the package because the information can be hiding somewhere in the label. When traveling to other countries, their rules about putting allergy information on packaging may be very different, so when traveling internationally, don't always trust labeling and do your research for that specific region.

I've learned that community is important to help keep people educated and safe. Hopefully this book helps educate you and makes you feel like you're part of my community as well!

There are many interesting facts in this book. For example, although I have nut allergies, I'm not allergic to coconuts because they are actually seeds. This is a common mistake because coconut has the word "**nut**" in it. Even though it's not really a nut, that doesn't mean I have to like the taste though. Did you know that peanuts also are not nuts? They are members of the pea family, they are legumes.

As you read this book, watch for call outs containing additional information for dealing with food allergies titled *Food Allergy Hacks and Tips*.

Lastly, I really appreciate your support. *50%* of all proceeds from this book will go toward helping fund research, programs, and technology to help make people with food allergies like you and me safer.

CHAPTER ONE

THE FIRST REACTION I REMEMBER

About three years ago, on a Friday, after school, I'd just left a bakery with my Mom, and we'd purchased a chocolate cream banana sandwich—sounds nice, huh? I'd never eaten there before, but thought that if I was careful, it would be fine. I asked the lady at the counter if the sandwich had any nuts in it, and explained that I was allergic to peanuts and tree nuts. She said the sandwich had no nuts in it, so I thought I was safe. Little did I know that the chocolate contained NUTELLA! DUN, DUN, DUNNNN!

Nutella is a delicious food spread, but it's also a hazelnut chocolate spread. It also has the word "nut" in it, like coconut, but unfortunately this wasn't a seed this time and actually has nuts in it. Nutella is now like a scary monster to me and I run whenever I'm near it.

I hopped in the car to have my first bite. It was delicious. It was so, so delicious. I remember it like it was yesterday. The chocolate melted in my mouth. Unfortunately, I started to feel a strange sensation, that my dad and I now call **'THE DEATH TINGLE'.**

I told my Mom that I felt really weird around my mouth and my throat was really scratchy. My Mom turned back from the front seat and immediately told me that I must be having an **allergic reaction**.

She quickly pulled the car over, examined my face, and called my father. We were close to a Pediatric Hospital, so we decided to meet there. This wasn't the best idea because you're supposed to call 911 and have an ambulance come right away, but my parents didn't know that at the time. My parents also didn't know they are supposed to give me the EpiPen® right away either.

We walked into the lobby of the hospital and checked in at the front desk. They did a quick examination and asked me to take a seat. Soon afterwards, my father arrived and began his mini-examination on me as well.

After he hastily looked me over, he decided he was going to stab me with the EpiPen®. In my mind, I was imagining a horror scene happening in the lobby of the hospital. At the time, I didn't think that the EpiPen® was necessary, so I looked for all the possible exits to plan my escape. I had never used the EpiPen® before this incident.

My dad is pretty fast though, so I tried to negotiate instead. I remember exactly what I said:

"Dad, Dad... I will give you **forty dollars** if you don't use the EpiPen®."

My dad laughed, he said it was funny because that was the most money I could think of at the time to change his mind. But to him, forty dollars wasn't worth the life of his son.

I realized all negotiations and pleading had failed. I had to resort to plan C, a.k.a. crying as loud as possible. There was also some begging involved.

Everyone waiting in the lobby was watching in anticipation of what was about to happen. It must have looked pretty funny to them, but it was not funny to me. My dad had had enough of the shenanigans. He held my leg, removed the safety on the EpiPen®, and jabbed it into my thigh.

I felt a sharp, burning pain, but it quickly went away. My dad didn't realize he needed to hold the EpiPen® tightly for ten seconds, so the spring jerked his hand back quickly away from my leg. The doctor said afterwards that it had still given me a good dose and had been effective in stopping my reaction.

The nurse came and took me to a hospital bed. Before long the doctor rushed in. After looking me over, they ran an IV (the thing they poke into your arm to give you medicine) and gave me a shot of **adrenaline** in my belly. Because I had swallowed the food, my body was still reacting. I needed to be monitored. I started to break out in hives. You can see the picture below:

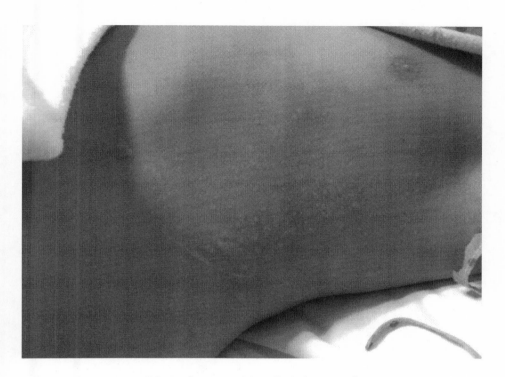

(Hives from my Nutella adventure)

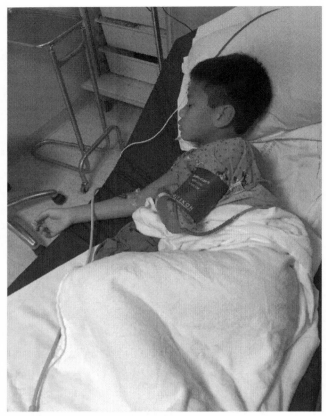

(IV and Blood Pressure Monitoring from my Hospital Visit)

I was monitored for about four hours, after which I was cleared to go home. My parents watched me for a while longer while I played video games, but, luckily, everything was fine.

I learned a very valuable lesson that day. I realized that if you have severe allergies you can't always trust people's word, even when preparing food is their job. I learned that it's always best to check the ingredients yourself, especially when away from home. In new scenarios, if you can't see the ingredient or get confirmation from a chef, it's best to avoid those foods all together if you have severe allergies. I also learned that hives really *sucks*!

CHAPTER TWO

UNDERSTANDING FOOD LABELS

Reading this chapter might help save your life or someone else's.

Becoming an expert label reader is **critical** for people with food allergies.

Health organizations and doctors emphasize how crucially important it is

to read labels. This chapter will help you identify allergens on labels and

avoid allergic reactions.

The diagram below shows where allergens are often listed on

food labels:

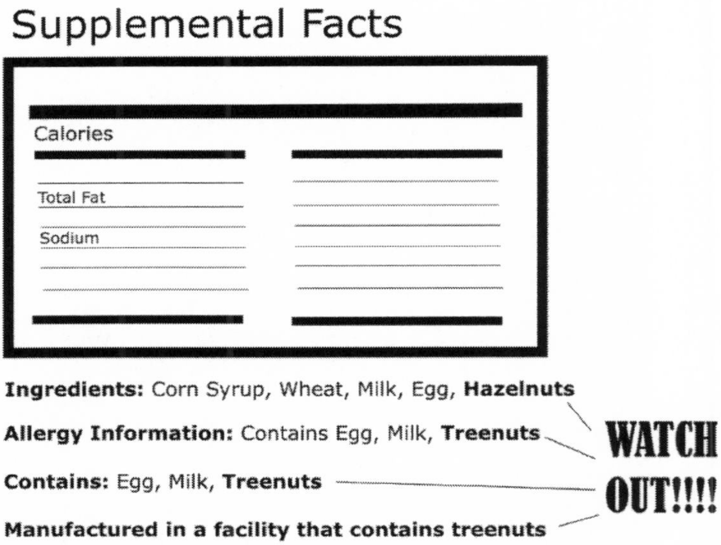

Supplemental Facts

Calories

Total Fat

Sodium

Ingredients: Corn Syrup, Wheat, Milk, Egg, **Hazelnuts**

Allergy Information: Contains Egg, Milk, **Treenuts**

Contains: Egg, Milk, **Treenuts**

Manufactured in a facility that contains treenuts

WATCH OUT!!!!

Allergens can be hiding on food labels, so be extra careful. You'll want to be sure to check all of the following sections:

- **Contains**

- **May Contain**

- **Ingredients**

- **Allergy Information**

- **Manufactured in a Facility**

 Food Allergy Hack

Always check all sections on food labels

The FDA (Food and Drug Administration) has stated that a specific fish, nut, or shellfish in foods must be declared on the label. Before you dig in, you should always check all of these sections—NO **MATTER WHAT!** Sometimes the "contains" section is not shown at all, so as a general rule, always check all the sections,

Another concern to watch out for when reading labels is cross-contamination. **Cross-contamination**, or cross-contact, can occur when allergens mix in via the manufacturing process, or come in contact with, an allergen free food—making it unsafe and dangerous. A small amount of an allergen can start an allergic reaction and cause swelling, hives, or other symptoms. Cross-Contamination can happen when foods come into contact with each other. For example, at buffets and potlucks where the food may become mixed with other foods. This is even possible when a serving utensil is used for serving more than one food item, so be cautious in these scenarios. If utensils are shared, we request they be washed. At ice cream shops, we request that the ice cream is served from their original containers in the back, instead of out of the public bins where cross-contamination may have occurred.

Here is a label for some cereal. See if you can find all the allergens. I've highlighted the "contains" section for this example:

INGREDIENTS: WHOLE OAT FLOUR, UNBLEACHED ENRICHED FLOUR (NIACIN, REDUCED IRON, THIAMINE MONONITRATE, RIBOFLAVIN, FOLIC ACID), SUGAR, YOGURT COATING (SUGAR, FRACTIONATED PALM KERNEL OIL, WHEY POWDER, WHOLE MILK POWDER, YOGURT POWDER [NONFAT DRY MILK, LACTIC ACID], TITANIUM DIOXIDE [WHITE COLOR], SOY LECITHIN [AN EMULSIFIER], SALT, NATURAL VANILLA FLAVOR), WHEAT STARCH, FREEZE-DRIED STRAWBERRIES, NATURAL FLAVORS, SALT, CALCIUM CARBONATE, SUNFLOWER OIL, SOY LECITHIN, SODIUM ASCORBATE, PURPLE/BLACK CARROT CONCENTRATE (COLOR), REDUCED IRON, NIACINAMIDE (VITAMIN B3), PYRIDOXINE HYDROCHLORIDE (VITAMIN B6), RIBOFLAVIN (VITAMIN B2), FOLIC ACID.

CONTAINS WHEAT, MILK, SOY. MAY CONTAIN TRACES OF TREE NUTS.

Notice that the "contains" section lists: "wheat, milk, soy, and may contain traces of tree nuts." This means that people with wheat, dairy, soy, and tree nuts allergies should avoid this food. "May contain" is stated because there is a chance that the food may have come in contact

21

with tree nuts during preparation or packaging. It's best to be on the safe side and avoid foods that list any severe allergens in the "may contain" section.

Also, notice that you should be able to find the allergen in the "ingredients" section. For example, the wheat allergen is listed as Wheat Oat Flour in the ingredients.

Okay, now that we have one out of the way, try to find the allergens on this label:

Nutrition Facts
Serving Size 1 tbsp (15mL)
Servings Per Container about 32

Amount Per Serving

Calories 5   Calories from Fat 0

% Daily Value*

Total Fat 0g	0%
Saturated Fat 0g	0%
Trans Fat 0g	
Cholesterol 0mg	0%
Sodium 0mg	0%
Total Carbohydrate 1g	0%
Dietary Fiber 0g	0%
Sugars 1g	
Protein 0g	

Vitamin A 0%   •   Vitamin C 0%
Calcium 0%   •   Iron 0%

*Percent Daily Values are based on a 2,000 calorie diet.

V Vegan

SHAKE WELL BEFORE USING
USE WITHIN 14 DAYS AFTER OPENING

INGREDIENTS:
ORGANIC COCONUT MILK (WATER, ORGANIC COCONUT CREAM), DRIED CANE SYRUP, DIPOTASSIUM PHOSPHATE, TITANIUM DIOXIDE (FOR COLOR), XANTHAN GUM.

CONTAINS COCONUT.

I hope you did your best, but if you didn't it is fine—no hard feelings! If you saw that the allergen is coconuts, think then about who can't eat this? Remember, earlier in the book we explained that coconuts are not a "nut", but a seed, so people with nut allergies *can* drink this beverage. This is important for people with nut allergies to understand.

Only if you have a coconut or seed allergy, should you avoid this drink.

If you have rare allergies, it can be even trickier to avoid a reaction because you'll see ingredient labels that list things like "natural flavoring and spices". Strawberries or watermelon are examples of common allergens that can be hiding in "natural flavoring", so be careful. You can always call the manufacture to verify if you really want to try a certain type of food, to learn whether it's safe or not.

Again, reading ingredients are very important to avoiding allergic reactions, at home or any place where you can see the labels. Even if you don't have allergies, you can help people with allergies that you know, and teach them how to read labels properly. Small things like reading the labeling can save a life or prevent someone from having a really bad day. I hope that this chapter has taught you to read label correctly, and to be able to apply to your life in a useful way.

You can learn more about product allergen labeling at the Food and Drug Administration website:

https://www.fda.gov/Food/GuidanceRegulation/GuidanceDocumentsRegulatoryInformation/Allergens/

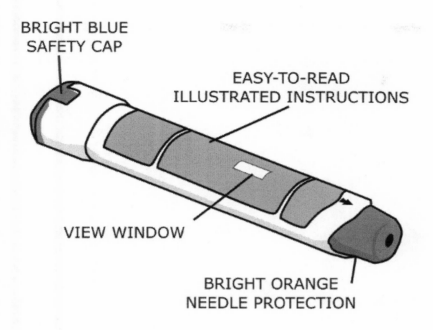

BRIGHT BLUE
SAFETY CAP

EASY-TO-READ
ILLUSTRATED INSTRUCTIONS

VIEW WINDOW

BRIGHT ORANGE
NEEDLE PROTECTION

C

HAPTER THREE

WHAT ARE EPIPENS® AND WHAT'S INSIDE?

EpiPens® are medical devices that stop your allergic reaction.

These devices have saved many lives. They are like super-heroes for

people with allergies. When you press and hold the EpiPen® against your

outer thigh, a needle injects *epinephrine*, also known as adrenaline, into your bloodstream. It is important to remove the blue safety off the top of the EpiPen® so that you can use it. When using the EpiPen®, hold it around the side; don't put your Thumb on the end. If you're holding it upside down, you might stab it through your thumb, *OUCH!!*

Make sure your doctor is aware of all your preexisting conditions when you get your first EpiPen®. You're supposed to administer the EpiPen® into the muscle of your outer thigh. The EpiPen® is fast-acting, it slows the allergic reaction, and it doesn't hurt. As you discovered from my first allergic reaction story, I used to be afraid of using the EpiPen®. Even recently, I struggled with using it immediately, which you'll learn about in my next embarrassing allergic reaction story. You should take the EpiPen® immediately if you think you've swallowed a dangerous allergen, then immediately call an ambulance. If you're a pig, make sure to call the hambulance. Sorry, I couldn't help myself.

DO NOT DRIVE YOURSELF TO THE HOSPITAL *unless there is no other option.* Seek immediately emergency attention by dialing 911, as the effects of the EpiPen® may wear off in as little as ten to twenty minutes, while an allergic reaction can last for hours and without further treatment may still be a serious threat.

Food Allergy Tip

Use your EpiPen® immediately after ingesting an allergen

if you have severe allergies

Food Allergy Tip

Always call 911 immediately after using your EpiPen®

Auto-Injector, as you may need to be monitored for

up to four hours

There is a spring that will push the needle away from the skin, so

you need to hold it firmly against the skin for 10 seconds. If it does

spring back, a good dosage has still entered the body. So, if your parent

insists on another dose, you can tell them you're probably okay with what you got already.

The window on the EpiPen® should be completely clear. If it's cloudy, then that EpiPen® has lost potency, due to temperature or other factors. Although it has lost potency, these EpiPens® are still better than nothing in an absolute emergency. You should, however, get that EpiPen® replaced as soon as you notice clouding. EpiPens® also have instructions on storage and expiration dates. Be sure to read this information and follow it appropriately.

If you're a kid who has multiple allergies, like me, you're more likely to need EpiPens® as it's much more likely you'll come in contact with allergens.

Epinephrine is a hormone commonly known as adrenaline. Hormones are used for organs in the body to communicate with one another. Epinephrine is created from the adrenal glands, which is located right above your kidneys. Just like all matter around us, epinephrine is a bunch of atoms connected together. Epinephrine is made of nine carbon atoms, three oxygen atoms, one nitrogen atom, and thirteen hydrogen atoms. You can see the chemical compound of epinephrine below:

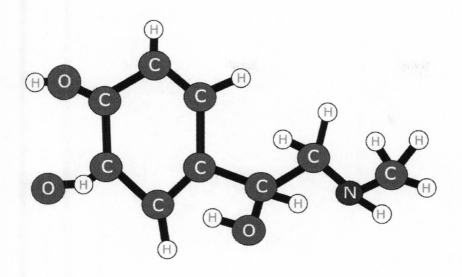

Epinephrine (a.k.a. adrenaline)

$C_9H_{13}NO_3$

(Carbon 9, Hydrogen 13, Nitrogen 1, Oxygen 3)

Like I said, epinephrine is naturally made in your adrenal glands. The adrenal glands can be found above your kidneys. You can see them in the diagram below:

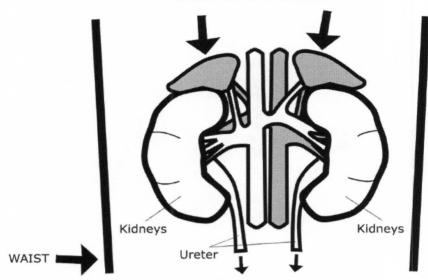

Adrenal Glands

Kidneys

WAIST

Ureter

Kidneys

Pee Goes to Your Bladder
from your kidneys

EpiPen® use can cause several common side effects:

- Sweating

- Nausea and Vomiting

- Pale Skin

- Feeling Short of Breath

- Dizziness

- Weakness

- Tremors (a body part may start to shake)

30

- Headache

- Feeling Nervous or Anxious

So, remember that an EpiPen® is a tool to help you, not to harm you. The EpiPen® injects epinephrine into your bloodstream to slow or stop an allergic reaction. Epinephrine is naturally made in the adrenal glands, located right above the kidneys. You push the EpiPen® into your outer thigh muscle. If you swallow an allergen, be brave, make sure to take your EpiPen® **immediately** and call 911.

CHAPTER FOUR

WHY IS MY BODY FREAKING OUT?

This chapter is about how and why your body is **freaking out** about foods that are harmless to most people. We'll talk about your immune system and how it reacts to allergens. In other words, this chapter is going to discuss why your body goes all wacky if you eat allergens.

The Immune System:

The purpose of the immune system is to protect the body from bacteria, viruses, fungi, and other microorganisms. The immune system is made up of organs that are collectively called the "lymphoid organs". These organs release "lymphocytes", which are white blood cells, or antibodies, to protect your body. A central part of the immune system is the **thymus**. The thymus is a lymphoid gland made of two same-sized lobes, located behind the sternum but in front of the heart. It derives its name from a resemblance it bears to the bud of the thyme plant.

The Thymus is the training area for **antibodies**. It learns what is and isn't a foreign invader as you grow up. The lymphatic system is a series of tubes and lymph nodes that carry white blood cells to different parts of the body.

Without an immune system, your body would be defenseless to foreign invaders. It saves our lives every day. Unfortunately, for those of us with food allergies, it occasionally puts our lives at risk by making mistakes, but it's still really good to have my immune system to keep us

33

safe and I'm really glad I have mine!

How Allergic Reactions Work:

When your immune system makes a mistake, it treats harmless foods as foreign invader. We aren't quite sure why our bodies choose to do this, but researchers are still learning a lot about the immune system so hopefully one day we'll know. When your body attacks these harmless foods, you can experience **anaphylaxis.**

Anaphylaxis, often called anaphylactic shock, happens when an allergen gets into your body and you have a **SEVERE REACTION.** Your immune system produces **histamines,** which bring blood and lymph fluid to the area. Histamine is a compound that is released by cells in response to injury. This, in turn, attracts **antibodies** to attack the invaders. Unfortunately, when it's a food allergy, your body is attacking itself along with the harmless food.

IgE (Immunoglobulin E) is an antibody that is produced by the immune system. When the body overreacts, Immunoglobulin E goes to the histamine where it releases its chemicals to attack what it believes is a foreign invader, thus starting an allergic reaction.

Although our body does a lot right to protect us, sometimes it gets it wrong. Understanding your immune system can help you understand what's going on in your body and recognize when something's not right.

Let's see how you're doing so far. Check out the crossword puzzle on the next page to test your knowledge:

Across:

1. _____ brings blood and lymph fluid to the area of the reaction.
2. _____ is the hormone found in an EpiPen.
8. Author is allergic to all _____.

Down:

3. Your _____ fights foreign invaders.
4. Food your body reacts negatively to is an _____.
5. A tool that injects epinephrine is an _____.
6. Food can cause an allergic _____.
7. The _____ is the training ground for antibodies.

So.... how did you do? Hopefully you remembered some of the terms related to food allergies. Now that we know a little bit more about reactions, let me share a story about my most recent allergic reaction.

Food Allergy Tip

Education on food allergies helps you understand your body and potential treatment options

CHAPTER FIVE

MOST RECENT REACTION, MANY MISTAKES

My most recent reaction was about three months ago on May 2017, and it was quite the... ummmm... *learning experience...* for me, and for my whole family. Although I try to be brave, it isn't always easy. It all started one day when we had pasta for dinner. Now, I know what you're thinking, why would pasta have nuts in it. **I was thinking the *same* thing!**

It's important to remember that often reactions happen far apart from each other, so you don't always remember the lessons from the last reaction. This happens for me because after a severe allergic reaction, I'm much more careful for a period of time, but after a while, it's easy to become careless. Also, when you have food allergies, you're not as frequently introduced to new foods.

The whole thing began when my mom and I sat at the dinner table. She had cooked a frozen ready-made pasta that was purchased from a popular grocer near our house. I had asked about nuts, and my mom had said it was safe.

Mistake Number #1:

I wasn't the one who checked the ingredients myself, even at home.

 *Food Allergy Hack*

Always check the ingredients yourself, even if a friend or family member says it's safe

---

I think you know how this played out. I took three small bites, and then I started to feel **THE DEATH TINGLE**. Queue the dramatic music.

I became upset, and let my mom know I was having a reaction. My father rushed downstairs. I took Benadryl and Claritin, but I didn't take the EpiPen®.

Mistake Number #2:

Didn't take the EpiPen® immediately after swallowing the allergen

---

To be honest, I broke a lot of important rules. My parents had me sit in the kitchen, so I could be monitored in a well-lit part of the house. I sat down, waiting for the medicine to take effect, while my parents argued in the dining area. I could hear them debating about whether to use the EpiPen® or not. After a few minutes, my dad realized my lips were swelling.

My dad grabbed the EpiPen®, and told my mom he was going to use it. A few moments later, I saw my dad walking towards me. He stared me in the eyes and said, "Kai, I'm going to use the EpiPen®."

Inside, I was ***freaking out!*** But then I noticed that he hadn't removed the safety from the EpiPen. Knowing the needle wouldn't deploy, I gave him a serious look and said, "Okay, Dad."

He reached up, and with one big stroke, pushed the EpiPen® against my thigh. Because the safety was still on, nothing happened. My dad seemed very confused. I tried to look like I was in pain, but it didn't work. He looked at me and asked, "am I supposed to take this blue piece off?"

Mistake Number #3:

My dad didn't remove the blue safety from the EpiPen® before

attempting to use it.

 *Food Allergy Tip*

Remember to remove the blue safety cap from your EpiPen® Auto-Injector before use

---

He pulled off the safety and that's when I really started to freak out.

I tried to take off running, but my dad wouldn't let me. I pleaded with him, "please don't do it!" All the intensity made my sister start running around crying as well. The whole house was losing it! He reached up again, holding my leg and jabbed the EpiPen® into my other thigh. This time, the needle deployed, but quickly recoiled, pushing the EpiPen, and my dad's hand, away from my leg. I stopped screaming, realizing that the EpiPen® didn't really hurt at all. I was really surprised. My father, however, didn't quite use it correctly.

Mistake Number #4:

My dad didn't hold the EpiPen® firmly against my outer thigh for ten seconds, so the recoil pushed the needle away from my leg.

Immediately after injecting the EpiPen®, my dad called the

ambulance. It arrived within five minutes. When they arrived, the paramedics asked some questions and examined me using a flashlight. They checked if I was still swelling, but it had already improved significantly. They advised my parents that I didn't need to go to the hospital this time but they should continue to monitor me even though the reaction was under control like they would at the hospital, especially when someone has swallowed an allergen since ingested allergens can continue to cause reactions while being digested.

Mistake Number #5:

People having allergic reactions should be monitored at home or at the hospital for 4 hours after ingesting an allergen, as the reaction can come back once the EpiPen® wears off.

Afterwards, we had a big family talk about safety, and agreed we shouldn't argue over the EpiPen® usage. This was an opportunity for us to get on the same page about when it's appropriate to use the EpiPen®. I learned that the EpiPen® doesn't really hurt, and it's a tool to save people's lives. I'm still a little afraid of the EpiPen®, but I know if I use it, it could save my life.

CHAPTER SIX

INTERESTING FACTS & STATISTICS

There is a bunch of great information about food allergies online and in other books. This chapter talks about some interesting facts related to food allergies that you may not already know. These facts are important because people with allergies can learn more about the people around them going through the same thing, and understand that they're not alone when dealing with food allergies. You'll come to find that many people deal with the same struggles throughout the world.

United States Statistics on Food Allergies:

Source: FoodAllergy.org

An estimated 15 million people have food allergies in the United States; that's about 1 in 13 people.

Every 3 minutes, a food allergy reaction sends someone to the emergency room (hopefully, this book will help reduce that number!).

More than 170 foods have been reported to cause allergic reactions. This means every day you likely eat something of which some kids are deathly afraid.

8 major food allergens are responsible for the majority of food allergies in the United State: Milk, Egg, Peanut, Tree Nuts, Wheat, Soy, Fish, and Crustacean Shellfish. I have two of eight major ones.

30 percent of children with food allergies are allergic to more than one food. (This surprised me personally; I thought kids with multiple allergies were rare because I haven't met many people with multiple allergies).

40 percent of children with food allergies experience severe allergic reactions, such as anaphylaxis. I didn't realize, before writing this book, that so many children have struggled to avoid severe reactions. Experiencing a life-threatening reaction is something a kid should ideally never have to go through.

Kids with food allergies are twice as likely to be bullied. Just because kids have allergies doesn't mean they should be treated differently.

Most fatal food reactions are triggered by food consumed

outside the home (This doesn't surprise me because at home,

it's easier to control of the ingredients and people tend to eat similar

types of food regularly).

Allergies to peanuts, tree nuts, fish and shellfish are generally lifelong. (I guess I'm just lucky that way!)

There was a 50% increase in the occurrence of childhood food allergies between 1997 and 2011. The cause isn't fully understood.

Source: World Health Organization

Worldwide, the prevalence of food allergies is estimated to be 3% of adults and 4-6% of children.

Awareness about food allergies among public food and health officials and among those supplying and preparing food is the first step in protecting all individuals with food allergies.

The clinical symptoms of food allergies range from mild discomfort to severe or life-threatening reactions which require immediate medical intervention.

Food Allergy Tip

Whenever you're frustrated with your allergies, like when you can't have cake at a birthday party, remember that you're not alone. Millions of other people have food allergies just in the United States alone.

Rare Types of Food Allergies:

There are many types of rare allergies around the world. I found some of these rare allergies to be interesting and thought I would share. Here is a list of some rare allergies: red meat, sesame seeds, avocados, marshmallows, corn, mango, coconut, spices, dried fruit, hot dogs, and pomegranates. I actually have food allergies to pomegranates, which is too bad because I really like pomegranates!

People can be allergic to things besides foods too; I have a family friend that is allergic to the cold! It's called "cold urticaria". Isn't that *interesting!?* As you can see, many people deal with moderate to severe allergies of many sorts. I hope you've found these facts useful and interesting. Being more informed helps you navigate your life with food allergies without feeling that you're doing it alone.

CHAPTER SEVEN

DOCTOR'S ADVICE ON AVOIDING

REACTIONS

In my opinion, you're never truly 100% safe from having a reaction without limiting your food choices drastically, but you can take several precautions to significantly lower the chances of having a reaction. In this chapter, I'll discuss a few things I do to avoid reactions, and advice from doctors I've interviewed about how people with allergies like you can be safe as well.

My Advice on Avoiding Reactions:

If you have severe food allergies, always check the ingredients! If you're ever in a restaurant, always ask for an allergy menu because some items can contain allergens when you least expect it. If they don't have an allergy menu, you should request that the waiter ask the chef if the dish you want has any of the allergens to which you're allergic.

If you're at a friend's house or at an event always check the ingredients extra carefully because in a new environment there are possibly new foods with new allergens. Many reactions happen away from home. If you have severe allergies, even if you're at your house and your parents or guardian know you have allergies, ask them if you can check the ingredients yourself. Ultimately, if you can't confirm the ingredients, it's safest to not eat the food.

Remember, if you're really eager to try a new food, but nervous, you can always call the manufacturer. Remember that the "May contain" statement on the label is optional for food companies and not required by law. It can be boring to read every ingredient, but especially with new foods you've never consumed, it is so important.

 **Food Allergy Tip**

Become an Expert Label Reader

Doctor's Advice:

Interview with Dr. Jon E. Welch, MD:

First, I want to thank Dr. Welch for taking the time to be interviewed for this book. He is rated a 5/5 on UCompareHealth and has over 20 years of experience in the field of immunology. Here's what he had to say:

What advice would you give kids with food allergies?

You have to be *very* careful about labels. Kids have to be taught that reading a label is important. There are allergens hidden in the food label, this is *absolutely critical to be aware of.*

What advice would you give parents?

Same advice, they have to be vigilant. The environments their kids will be in, such as day care, can be dangerous and unpredictable. They need to be careful and learn what is included in the standard meals at day cares or schools. They also have to be concerned about other kids having food in their lunch box that their kid is allergic to as well.

Anything interesting about research for food allergies?

It used to be that they would test people for allergies and if the results were consistent, then they would assign an EpiPen® and tell the patients and their parents to avoid the food.

What we now have is the ability to desensitize a person to their food allergies. No different than desensitizing people to bee allergies. This was a major step forward in treatment.

Thanks Dr. Welch!

Hopefully this information is helpful to you in avoiding having a reaction. It's easy to make a mistake, so like the doctor says, be vigilant! Like I say, always take things into your own hands when it comes to reading ingredients.

Keep safe snacks or meal replacement bars with you in case you can't eat any of the food at a location

CHAPTER EIGHT

ALLERGY TESTING AND COMMON TREATMENTS

The purpose of allergy testing is to identify the allergies that trigger an allergic reaction in your body, to understand the severity of your allergies, and to determine appropriate treatment. An allergy test usually involves a skin or blood test. If you know you're severely allergic to something, it's generally good to get tested for other allergens too, before you find out the hard way. Next, I'll discuss types of allergy tests as well as common treatments available today.

 **Food Allergy Tip**

Always keep an EpiPen® with you, and extra EpiPens® at school, home, and with your parents or guardians

Allergy Tests:

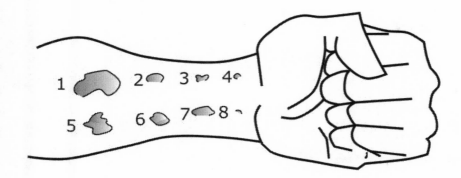

Skin Test:

   A skin test is used to check multiple potential allergens at once. This would in include airborne, food-related, and contact allergens. There are three type of skin tests: scratch, intradermal, and patch tests.

   Your doctor usually does a scratch test first. During a scratch test the allergen is put in liquid, then that liquid is placed on a section of your skin with a special tool that lightly inject the allergen into the skin's surface. You'll be closely monitored to see how your skin reacts to the allergen or substance. If there's redness, swelling, elevation, or itchiness of the skin over the test site, then you're likely allergic to that specific allergen.

If a scratch test is inconclusive, you will be given an intradermal test, which is when the allergen is injected into the dermis layer of your skin and, like the scratch test, you'll be monitored for any reactions.

Blood Test:

If there's a chance you'll have a severe allergic reaction to a skin test, your doctor may call for a blood test. The blood is tested in a laboratory for the specific antibodies that fight each type of allergen. This test is called an ImmunoCAP, and is very successful in detecting IgE antibodies to major allergens.

Elimination Diet:

An elimination diet is also something the doctor may try. An elimination diet may help your doctor determine which foods are causing you to have an allergic reaction if you have milder allergies. It entails removing certain foods from your diet and later adding them back in. Your reactions will help determine which foods cause problems.

The Results of Allergy Testing:

Once your doctor has determined which allergens are causing

your symptoms, you can work together to come up with a plan for avoiding them. Your doctor can also suggest medications that may ease your symptoms.

Common Treatments:

Antihistamines:

Antihistamine medicines block the action of the chemical histamine during an allergic reaction to an allergen. Histamine attracts the antibodies that cause your body to attack the allergen. Allergic symptoms, such as sneezing and itching, are not as bad when an antihistamine is taken.

Epinephrine:

Epinephrine, or adrenaline, is an injected medicine used to treat severe allergic reactions, breathing problems, and cardiac arrest. This is often injected by an EpiPen®. Epinephrine:

- Narrows the blood vessels, which raises blood pressure. This may prevent the severely low blood pressure that occurs during a severe allergic reaction.

- Stops leakage of fluids from blood vessels into body tissues.

- Relaxes the muscles of the respiratory tract, relieving wheezing and breathing difficulty.

- Increases heart rate.

Immunotherapy:

Immunotherapy can help your body get accustomed to allergens via exposure to small dosages. Immunotherapy isn't a cure quite yet, but in time your symptoms will get better and you may not have symptoms as often. This works well for people with a single allergy. For people with multiple severe allergies, as of right now, they would need to be desensitized to each allergen individually. Immunotherapy can be dangerous and is something you should **NEVER** try yourself.

A very recent four-year study found that combining desensitization and probiotics can accelerate tolerance, and potentially cure, Peanut allergies. This is an exciting area of research, and I would recommend asking your parents to check it out.

In summary, the purpose of allergy testing is to find what causes your allergic reactions and help prevent future reactions. Epinephrine is the common treatment for an allergic reaction. Immunotherapy is used to treat allergies and lessen the severity of your reaction. Taking these steps can identify your allergens, and stop reactions before life-threatening symptoms happen.

 **Food Allergy Tip**

If you haven't already, consider getting tested for different types of food allergens to prevent an unanticipated reaction in the future. Also, ask your doctor about desensitization treatment.

CHAPTER NINE

CONCLUSION

This book is meant to help kids with food allergies hear some stories and tips, become more educated on food allergies, and connect with communities of people dealing with the same struggles. I hope you have enjoyed this book and learned a lot along the way. We've discussed interesting facts, tips on avoiding reactions, EpiPens®, how to correctly read labels for food allergens, and advice from doctors who treat allergies and kids with allergies. I believe that through shared stories, education, and community, we can make the world a safer place.

The reason for my first reaction I described in Chapter One was that I didn't read the label on the food myself. I also didn't take the EpiPen®, and I didn't call the ambulance immediately.

In my second reaction story, I didn't read the label myself and relied on someone else to check for me. I also didn't take the EpiPen® immediately, until my dad stepped in and made me. These are common mistakes that are extremely dangerous.

As we discussed, EpiPens® are used in emergency situations, while other medicines like Benadryl and Claritin are for minor allergic reactions. In the EpiPen®, there is a dose of epinephrine to stop the reaction from sending you into anaphylactic shock.

In the allergy test section, there are three types of tests: skin, blood, and elimination diet. These tests are critical to helping you understand what allergens are dangerous to you.

There are several treatments to consider for our food allergies. With immunotherapy, a person is slowly exposed to an allergen little by little, lowering the severity of the reaction.

There was great advice from doctors and kids; the common thing they've said is to read labels and be careful in new environments. You've hopefully learned to read labels and tested your new knowledge in a fun book activity to make sure that you learned how to read label correctly. There were tips and more fun activities to entertain a young reader along this journey.

Thank you very much for taking the time to read my book. I truly appreciate it. Keep this book on hand and you can always reread it to refresh your memory. I've provided a check list below to remind you of the appropriate steps to take when you're having a serious reaction. I recommend cutting out the checklist and keeping it on your refrigerator.

Please share and recommend this book to others if you enjoyed it and found it helpful. Bye, and thank you so much for reading my book!

 *Food Allergy Hack*

If you're going to a birthday party, have your parents call a few days ahead to inform them of your allergies. This makes it much more likely you can enjoy some birthday cake!

Appendix

GREAT RESOURCES FOR KIDS

Check out these great resources for people dealing with food allergies!

http://www.kidsfan.org

On Twitter, follow #foodallergies and @kidsfanorg

https://www.foodallergy.org/

http://www.aafa.org/

http://www.epipen.com

http://www.kidswithfoodallergies.org

http://www.worldallergy.org

KFAN's FOOD ALLERGY CHECKLIST

QUICK, PRINTABLE

- HAVING A **REACTION**: EPIPEN® IMMEDIATELY. REMOVE SAFETY, PUSH INTO OUTER THIGH AND HOLD FOR 10 SECONDS. THEN, CALL 911

- **ALWAYS** READ INGREDIENTS AND LABELS FOR YOURSELF

- **ALWAYS** HAVE YOUR EPIPEN® AVAILABLE

- **SEARCH** FOR ALLERGENS IN SECTIONS LABELED "INGREDIENTS", "CONTAINS", "MAY CONTAIN" AND "MANUFACTURED" ON LABELING

- **ALWAYS** ASK THE **CHEF** TO VERIFY INGREDIENTS AT RESTAURANTS, DO NOT JUST RELY ON THE WAITING STAFF

- IF YOU CAN'T VERIFY INGREDIENTS, THE SAFE CHOICE IS: **DON'T EAT**

- DISCUSS **TREATMENT OPTIONS** WITH YOUR DOCTOR

Kids Food Allergy Network
http://kidsfan.org

CROSSWORD PUZZLE ANSWERS:

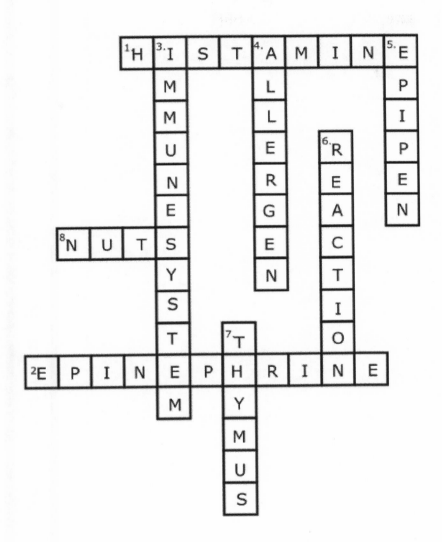

Made in the USA
Middletown, DE
02 August 2021